Faith That Prevails

Smith Wigglesworth

Gospel Publishing House/Springfield, Mo. 65802

02-0711

Contents

FAITH THAT PREVAILS
Copyright 1938, 1966 by the
Gospel Publishing House
Springfield, Missouri 65802

Printed in the United States of America

ISBN 0-88243-711-9

1

God-given Faith

Read Hebrews 11:1-11. I believe that there is only one way to all the treasures of God, and that is the way of faith. By faith and faith alone do we enter into a knowledge of the attributes, become partakers of the beatitudes, and participate in the glories of our ascended Lord. All His promises are Yea and Amen to them that believe.

God would have us come to Him by His own way. That is through the open door of grace. A way has been made. It is a beautiful way, and all His saints can enter in by this way and find rest. God has prescribed that the just shall live *by faith*. I find that all is failure that has not its base on the rock Christ Jesus. He is the only way, the truth and the life. The way of faith is the Christ way, receiving Him in His fulness and walking in Him; receiving His quickening life that filleth, moveth and changeth us, bringing us to a place where there is always an Amen in our hearts to all the will of God.

As I look into the 12th chapter of Acts, I find that the people were praying all night for Peter to come out of prison. They had a zeal but seem to have been lacking in faith.

They were to be commended for their zeal in spending their time in prayer without ceasing, but their faith, evidently, did not measure up to such a marvelous answer. Rhoda had more faith than the rest of them. When the knock came to the door, she ran to it, and the moment she heard Peter's voice, she ran back again with joy saying that Peter stood before the gate. And all the people said, "You are mad. It isn't so." But she constantly affirmed that it was even so.

Zacharias and Elisabeth surely wanted a son, but even when the angel came and told Zacharias that he should have a son, he was full of unbelief. And the angel said, "Thou shalt be dumb, because thou believest not my words."

But look at Mary. When the angel came to her, Mary said, "Be it unto me according to thy word." It was her Amen to the will of God. And God wants us with an Amen in our lives, an inward Amen, a mighty moving Amen, a God-inspired Amen, which says, "It is, because God has spoken. It cannot be otherwise. It is impossible to be otherwise."

Let us examine this 5th verse, "By faith Enoch was translated that he should not see death; and was not found, because God translated him: for before his translation, he had this testimony that he pleased God."

When I was in Sweden, the Lord worked

mightily. After one or two addresses the leaders called me and said, "We have heard very strange things about you, and we would like to know if they are true. We can see that God is with you, and that God is moving, and we know that it will be a great blessing to Sweden."

"Well," I said, "what is it?"

"Well," they said, "we have heard from good authority that you preach that you have the resurrection body." When I was in France I had an interpreter that believed this thing, and I found out, after I had preached once or twice through the interpreter, that she gave out her own ideas. And of course I did not know. I said to these brethren, "I tell you what my personal convictions are. I believe that if I had the testimony of Enoch I should be off. I believe that the moment Enoch had the testimony that he pleased God, off he went."

I pray that God will so quicken our faith, for translation is in the mind of God; but remember that translation comes on the line of holy obedience and a walk that is pleasing to God. This was true of Enoch. And I believe that we must have a like walk with God in the Spirit, having communion with Him, living under His divine smile, and I pray that God by His Spirit may so move us that we will be where Enoch was when he walked with God.

There are two kinds of faith. There is the natural faith. But the supernatural faith is the gift of God. In Acts 26:19, Paul is telling Agrippa of what the Lord said to him in commissioning him. "To open their eyes, and to turn them from darkness to light, from the power of Satan unto God, that they may receive forgiveness of sins, and inheritance among them which are sanctified by faith that is in Me."

Is that the faith of Paul? No, it is the faith that the Holy Ghost is giving. It is the faith that He brings to us as we press in and on with God. I want to put before you this difference between our faith and the faith of Jesus. Our faith comes to an end. Most people in this place have come to where they have said, "Lord, I can go no further. I have gone so far and I can go no further. I have used all the faith I have, and I have just to stop now and wait."

I remember being one day in Lancashire, and going round to see some sick people. I was taken into a house where there was a young woman lying on a bed, a very helpless case. The reason had gone, and many things were manifested there which were Satanic and I knew it. She was only a young woman, a beautiful child. The husband, quite a young man, came in with the baby, and he leaned over to kiss the wife. The moment he did, she threw herself over on the other side, just as a lunatic would do. That was very heart-breaking. Then he took the baby and pressed the baby's lips to the mother. Again another wild kind of thing happened. I asked one who was attending her, "Have you anybody to help?" "Oh," they said, "We have had everything." "But," I said, "have you no spiritual help?" Her husband stormed out, saying, "Help? You think that we believe in God, after we have had seven weeks of no sleep and maniac conditions."

Then a young woman of about eighteen or so just grinned at me and passed out of the door. That brought me to a place of compassion for the woman. Something had to be done, no matter what it was. Then with my faith I began to penetrate the heavens, and I was soon out of that house, I will tell you, for I never saw a man get anything from God who prayed on the earth. If you get anything from God, you will have to pray into heaven; for it is all there. If you are living in the earth realm and expect things from heaven, they will never come. And as I saw, in the presence of God, the limitations of my faith, there came another faith, a faith that could not be denied, a faith that took the promise, a faith that believed God's Word. And from that presence, I came back again to earth, but not the same man. God gave a faith that could shake hell and anything else.

I said, "Come out of her, in the name of Jesus!" And she rolled over and fell asleep and wakened in fourteen hours perfectly sane and perfectly whole.

There is a process on this line. Enoch walked with God. That must have been all those years as he was penetrating, and going through, and laying hold, and believing and seeing and getting into such close co-operation and touch with God that things moved on earth and he began to move toward heaven. At last it was not possible for him to stop any longer. Oh, Hallelujah!

In the 15th chapter of 1st Corinthians we read of the body being "sown in weakness," to be raised in power. It seems to me, that, as we are looking for translation, the Lord would have us know something of that power now, and would have us kept in that power, so that we shall not be sown in weakness.

There is one thing that God has given me from my youth up, a taste and relish for my Bible. I can say before God, I have never read a book but my Bible, so I know nothing about books. It seems to me better to get the Book of books for food for your soul, for the strengthening of your faith, and the building up of your character in God, so that all the time you are being changed and made meet to walk with God.

"Without faith it is impossible to please

Him; for he that cometh to God must believe that He is, and that He is a rewarder of them that diligently seek him."

I can see that it is impossible to please Him on any line but faith, for everything that is not of faith is sin. God wants us to see that the plan of faith is the ideal and principle of God. In this connection I love to keep in my thoughts the beautiful words in the 2nd verse of the 12th chapter of Hebrews: "Looking unto Jesus, the author and finisher of our faith." He is the author of faith. God worked through Him for the forming of the world. "All things were made by Him, and without Him was not anything made that was made." And because of the exceedingly abundant joy of providing for us so great salvation, He became the author of a living faith. And through this principle of living faith, looking unto Him who is the author and finisher of our faith, we are changed into the same image from glory to glory, even by the Spirit of the Lord.

God has something better for you than you have ever had in the past. Come out into all the fulness of faith and power and life and victory that He is willing to provide, as you forget the things of the past, and press right on for the prize of His high calling in Christ Jesus.

2

Like Precious Faith

Read 2 Peter 1:1-8. We are dull of comprehension because we so often let the cares of this world blind our eyes; but if we can be open to God, we shall see that He has a greater plan for us in the future than we have ever seen in the past. It is God's delight to make possible to us that which seems impossible, and when we reach a place where He alone has right of way, then all the things that have been misty and misunderstood are cleared up.

This *like precious faith* that Peter is writing about is a gift that God is willing to give to all of us, and I believe God wants us to receive it so that we may subdue kingdoms, work righteousness, and, if the time is come, to stop the mouths of lions. We should be able under all circumstances to triumph, because we have no confidence in ourselves, but our confidence is only in God. It is always those people who are full of faith that have a good report, that never murmur, that are in the place of victory, that are not in the place of human order but of divine order, since God has come to dwell in them.

This *like precious faith* is for all; but there may be some hindrance in your life that God will have to deal with. It seems to me as if I had had a thousand road engines come over my life to break me up like a potter's vessel. There is no other way into the deep things of God but a broken spirit. There is no other way into the power of God. God will do the exceeding abundantly above all we ask or think for us when He can bring us to the place where we can say with Paul, "I live no longer, and Another, even Christ, has taken the reins and the rule."

I understand God by His Word. I cannot understand God by impressions or feelings; I cannot get to know God by sentiments. If I am going to know God, I am going to know Him by His Word. I know I shall be in heaven, but I could not build on my feelings that I am going to heaven. I am going to heaven because God's Word says it, and I believe God's Word. And "faith cometh by hearing, and hearing by the Word of God." Rom. 10:17.

In Mark 11:24 we read, "What things soever ye desire, when ye pray, believe that ye receive them, and ye shall have them." The previous verse speaks of mountains removed, difficulties cleared away. Veneering won't do. We must have reality, the real working of our God. We must know God. We must be able to go in and hold converse with

God. We must also know the mind of God toward us, so that all our petitions are always on the line of His will.

As this *like precious faith* becomes a part of you, it will make you so that you will dare to do anything. And remember, God wants daring men, men who will dare all, men who will be strong in Him and dare to do exploits. How shall we reach this plane of faith? Let go your own thoughts, and take the thoughts of God, the Word of God. If you build yourself on imaginations you will go wrong. You have the Word of God and it is enough. A man gave this remarkable testimony concerning the Word: "Never compare this Book with other books. Comparisons are dangerous. Never think or never say that this Book contains the Word of God. *It is the Word of God*. It is supernatural in origin, eternal in duration, inexpressible in value, infinite in scope, regenerative in power, infallible in authority, universal in interest, personal in application, inspired in totality. Read it through. Write it down. Pray it in. Work it out. And then pass it on."

And truly the Word of God changes a man until he becomes an epistle of God. It transforms his mind, changes his character, moves him on from grace to grace, makes him an inheritor of the very nature of God. God comes in, dwells in, walks in, talks through, and sups with him who opens his being to the Word of God and receives the Spirit who inspired it.

When I was going over to New Zealand and Australia, I had many to see me off. There was an Indian doctor who was riding in the same car with me to the docks. He was very quiet and took in all things that were said on the ship. I began to preach, of course, and the Lord began to work among the people. In the second-class part of the ship there was a young man and his wife who were attendants on a lady and gentleman in the first-class. And as these two young people heard me talking to them privately and otherwise, they were very much impressed. Then the lady they were attending got very sick. In her sickness and her loneliness she could find no relief. They called in the doctor, and the doctor gave her no hope.

And then, when in this strange dilemma —she was a great Christian Scientist, a preacher of it, and had gone up and down preaching it—they thought of me. Knowing the conditions, and what she lived for, that it was late in the day, that in the condition of her mind she could only receive the simplest word, I said to her, "Now you are very sick, and I won't talk to you about anything save this; I will pray for you in the name of Jesus, and the moment I pray you will be healed."

And the moment I prayed she was healed. That was this like precious faith in operation. Then she was disturbed. Now I could have poured in oil very soon. But I poured in all the bitter drugs possible, and for three days I had her on cinders. I showed her her terrible state, and pointed out to her all her folly and the fallacy of her position. I showed her that there was nothing in Christian Science, that it is a lie from the beginning, one of the last agencies of hell. At best a lie, preaching a lie, and producing a lie.

Then she wakened up. She became so penitent and broken-hearted. But the thing that stirred her first was that she had to go to preach the simple gospel of Christ where she had preached Christian Science. She asked me if she had to give up certain things. I won't mention the things, they are too vile. I said, "What you have to do is to see Jesus and take Jesus." When she saw the Lord in His purity, the other things had to go. At the presence of Jesus all else goes.

This opened the door. I had to preach to all on the boat. This gave me a great opportunity. As I preached, the power of God fell, conviction came and sinners were saved. They followed me into my cabin one after another. God was working there.

Then this Indian doctor came. He said, "What shall I do? I cannot use medicine any more." "Why?" "Oh, your preaching has changed me. But I must have a foundation. Will you spend some time with me?" "Of course I will." Then we went alone and God broke the fallow ground. This Indian doctor was going right back to his Indian conditions under a new order. He had left a practice there. He told me of the great practice he had. He was going back to his practice to preach Jesus.

If you have lost your hunger for God, if you do not have a cry for more of God, you are missing the plan. There must come up from us a cry that cannot be satisfied with anything but God. He wants to give us the vision of the prize ahead that is something higher than we have ever attained. If you ever stop at any point, pick up at the place where you have dropped through, and begin again under the refining light and power of heaven and God will meet you. And while He will bring you to a consciousness of your own frailty and to a brokenness of spirit, your faith will lay hold of Him and all the divine resources; His light and compassion will be manifested through you, and He will send the rain.

Shall we not dedicate ourselves afresh to God? Some say, "I dedicated myself last night to God." Every new revelation brings a new dedication. Let us seek Him.

3

Spiritual Power

Bible Reading—Matthew 16.

The Pharisees and Sadducees had been tempting Jesus to show them a sign from heaven. He showed them that they could discern the signs that appeared on the face of the sky, and yet could not discern the signs of the times. He would give them no sign to satisfy their unbelieving curiosity, remarking that a wicked and adulterous generation sought after a sign, and that no sign would be given to them, but the sign of the prophet Jonah. A wicked and adulterous generation stumbles over the story of Jonah, but faith can see in that story a wonderful picture of the death, burial and resurrection of our Lord Jesus Christ.

After Jesus had departed from the Pharisees, and had come to the other side of the lake, He said to His disciples, "Take heed, and beware of the leaven of the Pharisees and of the Sadducees." The disciples began to reason among themselves; and all they could think of was that they had taken no bread. What were they to do? Then Jesus uttered these words, "O ye of little faith!" He had been so long with them, and yet they were still a great disappointment to

Him, because of their lack of comprehension and of faith. They could not grasp the profound spiritual truth He was bringing to them, and could only think about having brought no bread. "O ye of little faith! Do ye not yet understand, neither remember the five loaves of the five thousand, and how many baskets ye took up? Neither the seven loaves of the four thousand, and how many baskets ye took up?"

At one time Jesus said to Peter, "What thinkest thou, Simon? of whom do the kings of the earth take custom or tribute? of their own children or of strangers?" Peter said, "Of strangers." Then Jesus said, "Then are the children free. Nevertheless, lest we should offend them, go thou to the sea, and cast a hook, and take up the fish that first cometh up; and when thou hast opened his mouth, thou shalt find a piece of money; take that, and give unto them, for me and thee." Peter had been at the fishing business all his life, but he never had caught a fish with any silver in its mouth. But the Master does not want us to reason things out—for carnal reasoning will always land us in a bog of unbelief—but just to obey. "This is a hard job," Peter may have said, as he put the bait on his hook, "but since You told me to do it, I'll try;" and he cast his line into the sea. There were millions of fish in the sea, but every fish had to stand aside and leave that bait alone, and let that fish with the piece of money in his mouth come up and take it.

A woman came to me in Cardiff, Wales, who was filled with ulceration. She had fallen in the streets twice through this trouble. She came to the meeting and it seemed as if the evil power within her purposed to kill her right there, for she fell, and the power of the devil was rending her sore. She was helpless, and it seemed as if she had expired. I cried, "O God, help this woman." Then I rebuked the evil power in the name of Jesus, and instantly the Lord healed her. She rose up and made a great to-do. She felt the power of God in her body and wanted to testify all the time. After three days she went to another place and began to testify about the Lord's power to heal. She came to me and said, "I want to tell everyone about the Lord's healing power. Have you no tracts on this subject?" I handed her my Bible and said, "Matthew, Mark, Luke, John —they are the best tracts on healing. They are full of incidents about the power of Jesus. They will never fail to accomplish the work of God if people will believe them."

There is where men lack. All lack of faith is due to not feeding on God's Word. You need it every day. How can you enter into a life of faith? Feed on the living Christ of whom this Word is full. As you get taken up with the glorious fact and the wondrous presence of the living Christ, the faith of God will spring up within you. "Faith cometh by hearing, and hearing by the Word of God." Rom. 10:17.

Jesus asked His disciples what men were saying about Him. They told Him, "Some say that thou art John the Baptist; some, Elias; and others, Jeremias, or one of the prophets." Then He put the question, to see what they thought about it, "But whom say ye that I am?" Peter answered, "Thou art the Christ, the Son of the living God." And Jesus said to him, "Blessed art thou, Simon Bar-Jona: for flesh and blood hath not revealed it unto thee, but my Father which is in heaven." It is simple. Who do you say He is? Who is He? Do you say with Peter, "Thou art the Christ, the Son of the living God"? How can you know this? He is to be revealed. Flesh and blood does not reveal this. It is an inward revelation. God wants to reveal His Son within us and make us conscious of an inward presence. Then you can cry, "I know He is mine! He is mine! He is mine!" "Neither knoweth any man the Father, save the Son, and he to whomsoever the Son will reveal Him." Seek God until you get from Him a mighty revelation of the Son, until that inward revelation moves you on to the place where you are always steadfast, unmoveable, and always abounding in the work of the Lord.

There is a wonderful power in this revelation. "Upon this rock I will build my church; and the gates of hell shall not prevail against it. And I will give unto thee the keys of the kingdom of heaven; and whatsoever thou shalt bind on earth, shall be bound in heaven; and whatsoever thou shalt loose on earth shall be loosed in heaven." Was Peter the rock? No. A few minutes later he was so full of the devil that Christ had to say to him, "Get thee behind me, Satan; thou art an offense unto me." This rock was Christ. He is the Rock and there are many scriptures to confirm this. And to everyone who knows that He is the Christ He gives the key of faith, the power to bind and the power to loose. Stablish your hearts with this fact.

I had been preaching on this line in Toronto, endeavoring to show that the moment a man believes with all his heart God puts into him a reality, a substance, a life; yea, God dwells in him, and with the new birth there comes into us a mighty force that is mightier than all the power of the enemy. A man ran out of the meeting, and when I got home that night he was there with a big, fine, tall man. This man said to me, "Three years ago my nerves became shattered. I can't sleep. I have lost my business. I have lost everything. I am not able to sleep at all and my life is one of misery." I said to him, "Go home and sleep in the name of Jesus." He turned around and seemed reluctant to go; but I said to him, "Go!" and shoved him out of the door.

The next morning he rang up on the telephone. He said to my host: "Tell him I slept all night. I want to see him at once." He came and said, "I'm a new man. I feel I have new life. And now can you get me my money back?" I said. "Everything!" He said, "Tell me how." I said, "Come to the meeting tonight and I'll tell you." The power of God was mightily present in that evening meeting, and he was greatly under conviction. He made for the altar, but fell before he got there. The Lord changed him and everything in him. He is now a successful business man. All his past failures had come through a lack of the knowledge of God. No matter what troubles you, God can shake the devil out, and completely transform you. There is none like Him.

One day I was traveling in a railway train where there were two sick people in the car, a mother and her daughter. I said to them, "Look, I've something in this bag that will cure every case in the world. It has never been known to fail." They became very much interested, and I went on telling them more about this remedy that has never failed to remove disease and sickness. At last they summoned up courage to ask for a dose. So I opened my bag, took out

my Bible, and read them that verse, "I am
the Lord that healeth thee." It never fails.
He will heal you if you dare believe Him.
Men are searching everywhere today for
things with which they can heal themselves,
and they ignore the fact that the Balm of
Gilead is within easy reach. As I talked about
this wonderful Physician, the faith of both
mother and daughter went out toward Him,
and He healed them both, right in the train.

God has made His Word so precious that,
if I could not get another copy, I would not
part with my Bible for all the world. There
is life in the Word. There is virtue in it.
I find Christ in it; and He is the One I need
for spirit, soul and body. It tells me of the
power of His name and of the power of His
blood for cleansing. The lions may lack
and suffer hunger, but they that seek the Lord
shall not want any good thing. Psalm 34:10.

A man came to me at one time, brought
by a little woman. I said, "What's up with
him?" She said, "He gets situations, but he
fails every time. He is a slave to alcohol
and nicotine poison. He is a bright, intel-
ligent man in most things, but he goes under
to those two things." I was reminded of the
words of the Master, giving us power to bind
and loose, and I told him to put out his
tongue. In the name of the Lord Jesus Christ
I cast out the evil powers that gave him the
taste for these things. I said to him. "Man,

you are free today." He was unsaved, but when he realized the power of the Lord in delivering him, he came to the services, publicly acknowledged that he was a sinner, and the Lord saved and baptized him. A few days later I asked, "How are things with you?" He said, "I am delivered." God has given us the power to bind and the power to loose.

In another place a woman came to me and said, "I have not been able to smell for twenty years; can you do anything for me?" I said, "You shall smell tonight." Could I give anybody that which had been lost for twenty years? Not of myself, but I remembered the Rock on which God's church is built, the Rock Christ Jesus, and His promise to give to His own the power to bind and loose. We can dare to do anything if we know we have the Word of God behind us. In the name of the Lord Jesus I loosed this woman. She ran all the way home. The table was full of good things, but she would not touch a thing. She said, "I am having a feast of smelling!" Praise the Lord for the fact that He Himself backs up His own Word and proves the truth of it in these days of unbelief and apostasy.

Another person came and said, "What can you do for me? I have had sixteen operations and have had my ear drums taken out." I said, "God has not forgotten how to make ear drums." I anointed her and prayed, asking the Lord that the ear drums should be replaced. She was so deaf that I do not think she would have heard had a cannon gone off. She was as deaf afterwards as it was possible to be. But she saw other people getting healed and rejoicing. Has God forgotten to be gracious? Was His power just the same? She came the next night and said, "I have come tonight to believe God." Take care you do not come in any other way. I prayed for her again and commanded her ears to be loosed in the name of Jesus. She believed, and the moment she believed she heard, she ran and jumped upon a chair and began to preach. Later I let a pin drop and she heard it fall. God can give drums to ears. All things are possible with God. God can save the worst.

Discouraged one, cast your burden on the Lord. He will sustain you. Look unto Him and be lightened. Look unto Him now.

4

Paul's Pentecost

Read Acts 9:1-22.

Saul was probably the greatest persecutor that the early Christians had. We read that he made havoc of the church, entering into every house, and haling men and women, committed them to prison. At this time we find him breathing out threatenings and slaughter against the disciples of the Lord. He was on his way to Damascus for the purpose of destroying the church there. How did God deal with such a one? We should have dealt with him in judgment. God dealt with him in mercy. Oh, the wondrous love of God! He loved the saints at Damascus and the way He preserved them was through the salvation of the man who purposed to scatter and destroy them. Our God delights to be merciful and His grace is vouchsafed daily to both sinner and saint. He shows mercy to all. If we would but realize it, we are only alive today through the grace of our God.

More and more I see that it is through the grace of God that I am preserved every day. It is when we realize the goodness of God that we are brought to repentance. Here was Saul, with letters from the high priest, hastening to Damascus. He was struck

down and there came to his vision a light,
a light that was brighter than the sun. As
he fell speechless to the ground he heard a
voice saying to him, "Saul, Saul, why persecutest thou Me?" He answered, "Who art
thou, Lord?" And the answer came back,
"I am Jesus whom thou persecutest." And
he cried, "Lord, what wilt Thou have me
to do?" And the men that were with him lost
their speech—they were speechless—but they
led him to Damascus.

There are some people who have an idea
that it is only preachers who can know the
will of God. But the Lord had a disciple in
Damascus, a man behind the scenes, who
lived in a place where God could talk to him.
His ears were open. He was one who lis-
tened in to the things from heaven. Oh, this
is so much more marvelous than anything
you can hear on earth. It was to this man
that the Lord appeared in a vision. He told
him to go down to the street called Straight
and inquire for Saul. And He told him that
Saul had seen in a vision a man named
Ananias coming in and putting his hand on
him that he might receive his sight. Ananias
protested, "Lord, I have heard by many of
this man, how much evil he hath done to
Thy saints in Jerusalem: and here he hath
authority from the chief priests to bind all
that call on Thy name." But the Lord re-
assured Ananias that Saul was a chosen ves-

sel, and Ananias, nothing doubting, went on his errand of mercy.

The Lord had told Ananias concerning Saul, "Behold, he prayeth." Repentant prayer is always heard in heaven. The Lord never despises a broken and contrite heart. And to Saul was given this vision that was soon to be a reality, the vision of Ananias coming to pray for him that he might receive his sight.

As I was looking through my letters one day while in the city of Belfast, a man came up to me and said, "Are you visiting the sick?" He pointed me to a certain house and told me to go to it and there I would see a very sick woman. I went to the house and I saw a very helpless woman propped up in bed. I knew that humanly speaking she was beyond all help. She was breathing with short, sharp breaths as if every breath would be her last. I cried to the Lord and said, "Lord, tell me what to do." The Lord said to me, "Read the fifty-third chapter of Isaiah." I opened my Bible and did as I was told. I read down to the fifth verse of this chapter, when all of a sudden the woman shouted, "I am healed! I am healed!" I was amazed at this sudden exclamation and asked her to tell me what had happened. She said, "Two weeks ago I was cleaning house and I strained my heart very badly. Two physicians have been to see me, but they both told me there was no help.

But last night the Lord gave me a vision.
I saw you come right into my bedroom. I
saw you praying. I saw you open your
Bible at the fifty-third chapter of Isaiah.
When you got down to the fifth verse and
read the words, 'With His stripes we are
healed,' I saw myself wonderfully healed.
That was a vision, now it is a fact."

I do thank God that visions have not
ceased. The Holy Ghost can give visions,
and we may expect them in these last days.
God willeth not the death of any sinner and
He will use all kinds of means for their
salvation. Oh, what a gospel of love!

Ananias went down to the house on
Straight Street and he laid his hands on the
one who had before been a blasphemer and
a persecutor and he said to him, "Brother
Saul, the Lord, even Jesus, that appeared unto thee in the way as thou camest, hath sent
me, that thou mightest receive thy sight, and
be filled with the Holy Ghost." The Lord
had not forgotten his physical condition and
there was healing for him. But there was
something beyond this. It was the filling
with the Holy Ghost. Oh, it always seems
to me that the Gospel is robbed of its divine
glory when we overlook this marvelous truth
of the Baptism of the Holy Ghost. To be
saved is wonderful, to be a new creature, to
have passed from death unto life, to have the
witness of the Spirit that you are born of
God, all this is unspeakably precious. But

whereas we have the well of salvation bubbling up, we need to go on to a place where from within us shall flow rivers of living water. The Lord Jesus showed us very plainly that, if we believe on Him, from within us should flow rivers of living water.

God chose Saul. What was he? A blasphemer. A persecutor. That is grace. Our God is gracious and He loves to show His mercy to the vilest and worst of men. There was a notable character in the town in which I lived who was known as the worst man in the town. He was so vile, and his language was so horrible, that even wicked men could not stand it. In England they have what is known as the public hangman who has to perform all the executions. This man held that appointment and he told me later that he believed that when he performed the execution of men who had committed murder, that the demon power that was in them would come upon him and that in consequence he was possessed with a legion of demons. His life was so miserable that he purposed to make an end of life. He went down to a certain depot and purchased a ticket. The English trains are much different from the American. In every coach there are a number of small compartments and it is easy for anyone who wants to commit suicide to open the door of his compartment and throw himself out of the train. This man purposed to throw himself out of the train in a certain tunnel just as the train coming from an opposite direction would be about to dash past and he thought this would be a quick end to his life.

There was a young man at the depot that night who had been saved the night before. He was all on fire to get others saved and purposed in his heart that every day of his life he would get someone saved. He saw this dejected hangman and began to speak to him about his soul. He brought him down to our mission and there he came under a mighty conviction of sin. For two and a half hours he was literally sweating under conviction and you could see a vapor rising up from him. At the end of two and a half hours he was graciously saved.

I said, "Lord, tell me what to do." The Lord said, "Don't leave him, go home with him." I went to his house. When he saw his wife he said, "God has saved me." The wife broke down and she too was graciously saved. I tell you there was a difference in that home. Even the cat knew the difference.

There were two sons in that house and one of them said to his mother, "Mother, what is up in our house? It was never like this before. It is so peaceful. What is it?" She told him, "Father has been saved." The other son was struck with the same thing.

I took this man to many special services and the power of God was on him for many days. He would give his testimony and as he grew in grace he desired to preach the gospel. He became an evangelist and hundreds and hundreds were brought to a saving knowledge of the Lord Jesus Christ through his ministry. The grace of God is sufficient for the vilest and He can take the most wicked of men and make them monuments of His grace. He did this with Saul of Tarsus at the very time he was breathing out threatenings and slaughter against the disciples of the Lord. He did it with Berry the hangman. He will do it for hundreds more in response to our cries.

You will notice that when Ananias came into that house he called the one-time enemy of the gospel "Brother Saul." The Lord Jesus had sent Ananias to that house to put his hands upon this newly saved brother that he might receive his sight and be filled with the Holy Ghost. You say, "But it does not say that he spoke in tongues." We know that Paul did speak in tongues; that he spoke in tongues more than all the Corinthians. In those early days they were so near the time of that first Pentecostal outpouring that they would never have been satisfied with anyone receiving the Baptism unless they received it according to the original pattern given on the Day of Pentecost. When Peter was relating what took place in the house of Cornelius at Cæsarea he said, "And as I began to speak, the Holy Ghost fell on them, as on us at the beginning." Later, speaking of this incident, he said, "God, which knoweth the hearts, bear them witness, giving them the Holy Ghost, even as He did unto us; and put no difference between us and them, purifying their hearts by faith." And we know from the account of what took place at Cornelius' household that when the Holy Ghost fell "they heard them speak with tongues and magnify God." Many people think that God does make a difference between us and those at the beginning. But they have no Scripture for this. When anyone receives the gift of the Holy Ghost, there will assuredly be no difference between his experience today and that which was given on the Day of Pentecost. And I cannot believe that, when Saul was filled with the Holy Ghost the Lord made any difference in the experience that He gave him from the experience that He had given to Peter and the rest a short while before.

It was about thirty-one years ago that a man came to me and said, "Wigglesworth, do you know what is happening in Sunderland? People are being baptized in the Holy Ghost exactly the same way as the disciples were on the Day of Pentecost." I said, "I would like to go." I immediately took train and went to Sunderland. I went to the meetings and said, "I want to hear these tongues." I was told, "When you receive the Baptism in the Holy Ghost, you will speak in tongues." I said, "I have the Baptism in the Holy Ghost." One man said, "Brother, when I received the Baptism I spoke in tongues." I said, "Let's hear you." He could not speak in tongues to order, he could only speak as the Spirit gave him utterance and so my curiosity was not satisfied.

I saw these people were very earnest and I became quite hungry. I was anxious to see this new manifestation of the Spirit and I would be questioning all the time and spoiling a lot of the meetings. One man said to me, "I am a missionary and I have come here to seek the Baptism in the Holy Ghost. I am waiting on the Lord, but you have come in and are spoiling everything with your questions." I began to argue with him and our love became so hot that when we walked home he walked on one side of the road and I on the other.

That night there was to be a tarrying meeting and I purposed to go. I changed my clothes and left my key in the clothes I had taken off. As we came from the meeting in the middle of the night I found I did not have my key upon me and this missionary brother said, "You will have to come and sleep with me." But do you think we went to bed that night? Oh, no, we spent the night in prayer. We received a precious shower from above. The breakfast bell rang, but that was nothing to me. For four days I wanted nothing but God. If you only knew the unspeakably wonderful blessing of being filled with the Third Person of the Trinity, you would set aside everything else to tarry for this infilling.

I was about to leave Sunderland. This revival was taking place in the vestry of an Episcopal Church. I went to the Vicarage that day to say good-bye and I said to Sister Boddy, the vicar's wife, "I am going away, but I have not received the tongues yet." She said, "It isn't tongues you need, but the Baptism." I said, "I have the Baptism, Sister, but I would like to have you lay hands on me before I leave." She laid her hands on me and then had to go out of the room. The fire fell. It was a wonderful time as I was there with God alone. It seemed as though God bathed me in power. I was given a wonderful vision. I was conscious of the cleansing of the precious blood and cried out, "Clean! Clean! Clean!" I was filled with the joy of the consciousness of the cleansing. I saw the Lord Jesus Christ. I saw the empty cross and I saw Him exalted at the right hand of God the Father. As I was extolling, magnifying, and praising Him I was speaking in tongues as the Spirit of God gave me utterance. I knew now that I had received the real Baptism in the Holy Ghost.

I sent a telegram home and when I got there one of our boys said, "Father, I hear you have been speaking in tongues. Let's hear you." I could not speak in tongues.

I had been moved to speak in tongues as the Spirit of God gave utterance at the moment I received the Baptism, but I did not receive the gift of tongues and could not speak a word. I never spoke again in tongues until nine months later when I was praying for someone, and it was then that God gave me the permanent gift of speaking in tongues.

And so Saul was filled with the Holy Ghost and in the later chapters of the Acts of the Apostles we see the result of this infilling. Oh, what a difference it makes. When I got home my wife said to me, "So you think you have received the Baptism of the Holy Ghost. Why, I am as much baptized in the Holy Ghost as you are." We had sat on the platform together for twenty years but that night she said, "Tonight you will go by yourself." I said, "All right." As I went up to the platform that night the Lord gave me the first few verses of the sixty-first chapter of Isaiah, "The Spirit of the Lord God is upon me; because the Lord hath anointed me to preach good tidings unto the meek: He hath sent me to bind up the broken-hearted, to proclaim liberty to the captives, and the opening of the prison to them that are bound." My wife went back to one of the furthermost seats in the hall and she said to herself, "I will watch it." I preached that night on the subject the Lord had given me and I told what the Lord had done for me. I told the people that I was

going to have God in my life and I would
gladly suffer a thousand deaths rather than
forfeit this wonderful infilling that had come
to me.   My wife was very restless.   She was
moved in a new way and said, "That is not
my Smith that is preaching.   Lord, you have
done something for him."   As soon as I had
finished, the secretary of the mission got up
and said, "Brethren, I want what the leader
of our mission has got."   He tried to sit
down but missed his seat and fell on the
floor.   There were soon fourteen of them on
the floor, my own wife included.   We did
not know what to do, but the Holy Ghost
got hold of the situation and the fire fell.   A
revival started and the crowds came.   It was
only the beginning of the flood-tide of blessing.   We had touched the reservoir of the
Lord's life and power.   Since that time the
Lord has taken me to many different lands
and I have witnessed many blessed outpour-
ings of God's Holy Spirit.

The grace of God that was given to the
persecuting Saul is available for you.   The
same Holy Ghost infilling he received is like-
wise available.   Do not rest satisfied with
any lesser experience than the Baptism that
the disciples received on the Day of Pentecost, then move on to a life of continuous
receiving of more and more of the blessed
Spirit of God.

5

Ye Shall Receive Power

"Ye shall receive power after the Holy Ghost is come upon you." The disciples had been asking whether the Lord would at that time restore again the kingdom to Israel. Christ told them that it was not for them to know the times and seasons which the Father had put in His own power, but He promised them that when they received the Holy Ghost they should receive power to witness for Him in all the world. To receive the Holy Ghost is to receive power with God, and power with men.

There is a power of God and there is a power which is of Satan. When the Holy Spirit fell in the early days, a number of spiritists came to our meetings. They thought we had received something like they had and they were coming to have a good time. They filled the two front rows of our mission. When the power of God fell, these imitators began their shaking and muttering under the power of the devil. The Spirit of the Lord came mightily upon me and I cried. "Now, you devils, clear out of this!" And out they went. I followed them right out into the street and then they turned round and cursed me. There was power from below, but it was no match for the power of the Holy Ghost, and they soon had to retreat.

The Lord wants all saved people to receive power from on High—power to witness, power to act, power to live, and power to show forth the divine manifestation of God within. The power of God will take you out of your own plans and put you into the plan of God. You will be unmantled and divested of that which is purely of yourself and put into a divine order. The Lord will change you and put His mind where yours was, and thus enable you to have the mind of Christ. Instead of your laboring according to your own plan, it will be God working in you and through you to do His own good pleasure through the power of the Spirit within. Someone has said that you are no good until you have your "I" knocked out. Christ must reign within, and the life in the Holy Ghost means at all times the subjection of your own will to make way for the working out of the good and acceptable and perfect will of God within.

I was holding a meeting, once, in London, and at the close a man came to me and said, "We are not allowed to hold meetings in this hall after 11 o'clock, and we would like you to come home with us, I am so hungry for God." The wife said she, too, was hungry, and so I agreed to go with them. At about 12:30 we arrived at their house. The man began stirring up the fire and said, "Now we will have a good supper." I said to them, "I did not come here for your warm fire, your supper or your bed. I came here because I thought you were hungry to get more of God." We got down to pray and at about 3:30 the Lord baptized the wife, and she spoke in tongues as the Spirit gave utterance. At about 5 o'clock I spoke to the husband and asked how he was getting on. He replied, "God has broken my iron, stubborn will." He had not received the Baptism, but God had wrought a mighty work within him.

The following day, at his business, everyone could tell that a great change had come to him. Before he had been a walking terror. The men who labored for him had looked upon him as a regular devil because of the way he had acted; but coming into contact with the power of God that night completely changed him. Before this he had made a religious profession, but he had never truly entered into the experience of the new birth until that night, when the power of God surged so mightily through his home. A short while afterwards I went to this man's home, and his two sons ran to me and kissed me, saying "We have a new father." Previous to this these boys had often said to their mother, "Mother, we cannot stand it in the home any longer. We will have to leave." But the Lord changed the whole situation that night as we prayed together. On the second visit the Lord baptized this man in the Holy Ghost. The Holy Spirit will reveal false positions, pull the mask off any refuge of lies and clean up and remove all false conditions. When the Holy Spirit came in, that man's house and business and he himself were entirely changed.

When the Holy Spirit comes He comes to empower you to be an effective witness. At one time we were holding some special meetings and I was out distributing bills. I went into a shoemaker's store and there was a man with a green shade over his eyes and also a cloth. My heart looked up to the Lord and I had the witness within that He was ready to change any condition. The man was crying, "Oh! Oh!! Oh!!! I asked, "What's the trouble?" He said he was suffering with great inflammation and burning. I said, "I rebuke this condition in Jesus' name." Instantly the Lord healed him. He took off the shade and cloth and said, "Look, it is all gone."

At one time a lady wrote and asked if I could go and help her. She said that she was blind, having two blood clots behind her eyes. When I reached the house they brought the blind woman to me. We were together for some time and then the power of God fell. Rushing to the window she exclaimed, "I can see! Oh, I can see! The blood is gone, I can see." She then inquired about receiving the Holy Spirit and confessed that for ten years she had been fighting our position. She said, "I could not bear these tongues, but God has settled the whole thing today. I now want the Baptism in the Holy Ghost." The Lord graciously baptized her in the Spirit.

The Holy Spirit will come when a man is cleansed. There must be a purging of the old life. I never saw anyone baptized who was not clean within.

I remember being in a meeting at one time, where there was a man seeking the Baptism, and he looked like he was in trouble. He was very restless, and finally he said to me, "I will have to go." I said, "What's up?" He said, "God is unveiling things to me, and I feel so unworthy." I said, "Repent of everything that is wrong." He continued to tarry and the Lord continued to search his heart. These times of waiting on God for the fullness of the Spirit are times when He searches the heart and tries the reins. Later the man said to me, "I have a hard thing to do, the hardest thing I have ever had to do." I said to him, "Tell the Lord you will do it, and never mind the consequences."

He agreed, and the next morning he had to take a ride of thirty miles and go with a bag of gold to a certain party with whom he dealt. This man had a hundred head of cattle and he bought all his feed at a certain place. He always paid his accounts on a certain day, but one day he missed. He was always so punctual in paying his accounts that when later the people of his firm went over their books, they thought they must have made a mistake in not crediting the man with the money and so they sent him a receipt. The man never intended not to pay the account, but if you defer to do a right thing the devil will see that you never do it. But when that man was seeking the Lord that night the Lord dealt with him on this point, and he had to go and straighten the thing the next morning. He paid the account and then the Lord baptized him in the Spirit. They that bear the vessels of the Lord must be clean, must be holy.

When the Holy Spirit comes He always brings a rich revelation of Christ. Christ becomes so real to you that, when, under the power of the Spirit, you begin to express your love and praise to Him, you find yourself speaking in another tongue. Oh, it is a wonderful thing! At one time I belonged to a class who believed that they had received the Baptism in the Spirit without the speaking in tongues. There are many folks like that today, but if you can go with them to a prayer meeting you will find them asking the Lord again and again to baptize them in the Spirit. Why all this asking if they really have received the Baptism? I have never heard anyone who has received the Baptism in the Holy Ghost after the original pattern asking the Lord to give them the Holy Ghost. They know of a surety that He has come.

I was once traveling from Belgium to England. As I landed I received a request to stop at a place between Harwich and Colchester. The people were delighted that God had sent me, and told me of a special case they wanted me to pray for. They said, "We have a brother here who believes in the Lord, and he is paralyzed from his loins downward. He cannot stand on his legs and he has been twenty years in this condition." They took me to this man and as I saw him there in his chair I put the question to him. "What is the greatest desire in your heart?" He said, "Oh, if I could only receive the Holy Ghost!" I was somewhat surprised at this answer, and I laid my hands on his head and said, "Receive ye the Holy Ghost." Instantly the power of God fell upon him and he began breathing very heavily. He rolled off the chair and there he lay like a bag of potatoes, utterly helpless. I like anything that God does. I like to watch

God working. There he was with his great, fat body, and his head was working just as though it was on a swivel. Then to our joy he began speaking in tongues. I had my eyes on every bit of him and as I saw the condition of his legs I said, "Those legs can never carry that body." Then I looked up and said, "Lord, tell me what to do." The Holy Ghost is the executive of Jesus Christ and the Father. If you want to know the mind of God you must have the Holy Ghost to bring God's latest thought to you and to tell you what to do. The Lord said to me, "Command him in My name to walk." But I missed it, of course. I said to the people there, "Let's see if we can lift him up." But we could not lift him, he was like a ton weight. I cried, "Oh Lord, forgive me." I repented of doing the wrong thing, and then the Lord said to me again, "Command him to walk." I said to him, "Arise in the name of Jesus." His legs were immediately strengthened. Did he walk? He ran all round. A month after this he walked ten miles and back. He has a Pentecostal work now. When the power of the Holy Ghost is present, things will happen.

6

Keeping the Vision

Read the 20th chapter of the Acts of the Apostles, beginning at verse 7. Humanity is a failure everywhere. But when humanity is filled with divine power, there is no such thing as failure; and we know that the Baptism of the Holy Spirit is not a failure.

There are two sides to this Baptism: the first is, that you possess the Spirit; the second is that the Spirit possesses you. This is my message at this time—*being possessed by the Baptizer,* and not merely possessing the Baptizer. There is no limit to the possibilities of such a life, because it has God behind it, in the midst of it, and through it. I see people from time to time very slack, cold, and indifferent; but after they get filled with the Holy Spirit they become ablaze for God. I believe that God's ministers are to be flames of fire; nothing less than flames; nothing less than mighty instruments with burning messages, with a heart full of love, with such a depth of consecration that God has taken full charge of the body and it exists only that it may manifest the glory of God. Surely, this is the ideal and the purpose of this great plan of salvation for man—that we might be filled with all the fulness of God, and become ministers of life, God working mightily in us and through us to manifest His grace—the saving power of humanity.

Now let us turn to this wonderful Word of God. I want you to see the demonstration of this power in this man Paul—this man who was "born out of due time;" this Paul, who was plucked as a brand from the burning; this Paul whom God chose to be an apostle to the Gentiles. See him first as a persecutor, mad to destroy those who were bringing glad tidings to the people. See how madly he rushed those people to prison, striving to make them blaspheme that holy name. Then see this same man changed by the power of God and the Gospel of Christ; see him filled with the Holy Ghost, becoming a builder for God and a revealer of the Son of God, so that he could say, "It is no longer I that live, but Christ liveth in me." Gal. 2:20.

In the 9th chapter of Acts, we read that he was called to a special ministry. The Lord said to Ananias, "I will show him what great things he must suffer for my name's sake." I don't want you to think that this means suffering from diseases; for it means suffering persecution, suffering from slander, from strife, from bitterness, from revilings and from many other evil things; but none of these things will hurt you; rather, they will kindle the fire of holy ambition, because the scripture says, "Blessed are they that have been persecuted for righteousness' sake: for theirs is the kingdom of heaven." Matt. 5:10. To be persecuted for Christ's sake is to be joined up with a blessed, blessed people; but, better still, it means to be united with our Lord Jesus in the closest of fellowship, the fellowship of His suffering. There is a day coming when we will rejoice greatly that we have been privileged to suffer for His name's sake.

Beloved, God wants witnesses, witnesses to the truth, witnesses to the full truth, witnesses to the fulness of redemption—deliverance from sin and deliverance from disease—by the eternal power working in them, as they are filled with life through the Spirit. God wants us to believe that we may be ministers of that kind—of glorious things wrought in us by the Holy Spirit.

See in verse 7, how Paul was lost in his zeal for his ministry, so that he "continued his speech until midnight." Then something happened that threatened to break up the meeting—a young man, becoming sleepy, fell out of the window. That was enough to break up any ordinary meeting. But this man, filled with the Spirit of God, was equal even to such an emergency even on the moment. He went down, picked up the young man, brought life back into him by the

Spirit of life that was in him, then returned
to the upper room and continued the meeting
until break of day.

In Switzerland the people said to me,
"How long can you preach to us?" I said to
them, "When the Holy Ghost is upon us, we
can preach forever!" When I was in San
Francisco, driving down the main street one
day, we came across a crowd in the street. The
driver stopped and I jumped out of the car,
and right across from where the tumult was,
I found a boy lying on the ground apparent-
ly in the grip of death. I got down and asked,
"What is amiss?" He replied in a whisper,
"tramp." I put my hand underneath his
back and said, "In the name of Jesus, come
out." And the boy jumped up and ran away,
not even stopping to say, "Thank you."

So you will find out that, with the Baptism of the Holy Spirit, you will be in a
position to act when you have no time to
think. The power and working of the Holy
Spirit is of divine origin. It is the supernatural, God thrilling and moving one with
the authority and power of almightiness, and
it brings things to pass that could not come
to pass in any other way. I had some things
of this character happen on the ship as I was
crossing the ocean. I want ever to be in
Paul's position—that at any time, even at
midnight, in the face of anything, even death
itself, God may be able to manifest His

power and do what He wants to do through me. This is what it means to be possessed by the Spirit of God. My heart is thrilled with the possibility of coming into the place where Paul was. Let us read verse 19, that we may get our mind perfectly fortified with this blessed truth that God has for us.

"Serving the Lord with all humility of mind." None of us is going to be able to be a minister of this new covenant of promise in the unction and power of the Spirit without humility. It seems to me that the way to get up is to get down. It is clear to me that in the measure that the dying of the Lord is in me, the life of the Lord will abound in me. And to me, truly, a Baptism of the Holy Spirit is not the goal, but it is an inflow to reach the highest level, the holiest position that it is possible for human nature to reach by Divine power. The Baptism of the Holy Spirit is given to reveal and to make real Him in whom dwells "all the fulness of the Godhead bodily." Col. 2:9. So I see that to be baptized in the Holy Spirit means to be baptized into death, into life, into power, into fellowship with the Trinity, where the old life ceases to be, and the life of God possesses us forever.

No man can live after seeing God; and God wants us all to see Him in all His glorious, infinite sufficiency, so that we shall joyfully cease to be—that He may become our life.   Thus it was that Paul could say, "It is no longer I that live, but Christ liveth in me." I believe that God wants to make real to us all this ideal of humility where we so recognize human helplessness and human insufficiency that we shall rest no more on human plans and human devices and human energy, but continually look to God for His thought, for His voice, for His power, for His all-sufficiency in all things.

Now here is another word for us. Let us read it. It is found in verse 22. "Now, behold, I go bound in spirit." Is there a possibility of the human so coming into oneness with the divine will? Let me give you two other versions of Scripture. Jesus was a man of flesh and blood like ourselves; though He was the incarnation of the authority and power and majesty of heaven, yet He bore about in His body our flesh, our human weakness, being tempted in all points like as we are, yet without sin. Oh, He was so lovely! Such a perfect Saviour! Oh, that I could shout "Jesus!" so that all the world would hear. There is salvation, life, power, and deliverance through that name; but, beloved, I read in Mark 1:12, that that body was driven by the Spirit. In the fourth chapter of Luke, it says "led" by the Spirit. And now here is Paul "bound" in the spirit.

Oh, what condescension that God should lay hold of humanity and so possess it with

His holiness, with His righteousness, with His truth, with His faith, that we can say: "I am bound in spirit; I have no choice; my only choice is for God; my only desire, my only ambition is the will of God; I am bound with God." Is this possible, beloved? If you look into Galatians, first chapter, you will see how wonderfully Paul rose into this state of bliss. If you look in the third chapter of the Ephesians, you will see that he recognized himself as less than the least of all saints. Then, if you'll look into the 26th chapter of Acts, you will find him saying, "I have never lost the vision, King Agrippa, I have never lost it." Then if you will look again in Galatians, you will see that, in order to keep the vision, he conferred not with flesh and blood; God laid hold of him, God bound him, God preserved him. I ought to say, however, that it is a wonderful position to be in—to be preserved by Almightiness—and we ought to see to it that we leave ourselves to God. The consequences will be all right. "Whosoever shall seek to save his life, shall lose it; and whoever shall lose his life for my sake the same shall save it."

Now, beloved, I am out for men. It is my business to be out for men. It is my business to make everybody hungry, dissatisfied. It is my business to make people either glad or mad. I have a message from heaven that will not leave people as I find them.

Something must happen after they are filled with the Holy Spirit. A man filled with the Holy Spirit is no longer an ordinary man. A man can be swept by the power of God in the first stage of the revelation of Christ so that from that moment he will be an extraordinary man. But to be filled with the Holy Spirit he has to become a free body for God to dwell in, and to use, and to manifest Himself through. So I appeal to you, you people who have received the Holy Spirit, I appeal to you to let God have His way at whatever cost; I appeal to you to keep moving on with God into an ever increasing realization of His infinite purpose in Christ Jesus for His redeemed ones until you are filled unto all the fulness of God. To remain three days in the same place would indicate that you had lost the vision. The child of God must catch the vision anew every day. Every day the child of God must be moved more and more by the Holy Ghost. The child of God must come into line with the power of heaven so that he knows that God has His hand upon him.

It is the same Jesus, the very same Jesus. He went about doing good. "God anointed Him with the Holy Ghost and with power: who went about doing good, and healing all that were oppressed of the devil; for God was with Him." Beloved, is not that the ministry that God would have us see we are heir to? The mission of the Holy Ghost is to give us a revelation of Jesus and to make the Word of God life unto us as it was when spoken by the Son—as new, as fresh, as effective as if the Lord Himself were speaking. The Bride loves to hear the Bridegroom's voice! Here it is, the blessed Word of God, the whole Word, not part of it, no, no, no! We believe in the whole of it. We really have such an effectiveness worked in us by the Word of life, that day by day we are finding out that the Word itself giveth life; the Spirit of the Lord, breathing through, revealing by the Word, giving it afresh to us, makes the whole Word alive today. Amen. So I have within my hands, within my heart, within my mind, this blessed reservoir of promises that is able to do so many marvelous things. Some of you most likely have been suffering because you have a limited revelation of Jesus, of the fulness of life there is in Him.

In Oakland, Calif., we had a meeting in a large theater. God wrought in filling the place till we had to have overflow meetings. There was a rising tide of people getting saved in the meeting by rising voluntarily up and down in the place, and getting saved. And then we had a rising tide of people who needed help in their bodies, rising in faith and being healed. One of these latter was an old man 95 years of age. He had been suffering

for three years, till he got to the place where
for three weeks he had been taking liquids.
He was in a terrible state. I got him to stand
while I prayed for him; and he came back,
and, with radiant face, told us that new
life had come into his body. He said, "I am
95 years old. When I came into the meeting, I was full of pain from cancer of the
stomach. I have been so healed that I have
been eating perfectly, and have no pain."
Many of the people were healed in a similar
way.

(After the telling of the above incident
in the meeting in Wellington, New Zealand,
where this address was given, a lady arose
who had rheumatism in the left leg. After
being prayed for, she ran the full length of
the hall several times, then testified to partial
healing. A young man with pain in the
head was healed instantly. Another man
with pain in the shoulder was healed instantly also.)

In the second chapter of Acts, you will
see that when the Holy Ghost came there
was such a manifestation of the power of
God that it wrought conviction as the Word
was spoken in the Holy Ghost. In the third
chapter we read of the lame man healed at
the Beautiful Gate through the power of the
Spirit, as Peter and John went into the
Temple. And in the fourth chapter, we read
of such a wonderful manifestation of mira-

culous power through the Spirit that five thousand men besides women and children became believers in the Lord Jesus Christ. God gives manifestation of His Divine power, beloved, to prove that He is with us. Will you not, right now, open your heart to this wonderful God, and let Him come into your life and make of you all that His infinite wisdom has conceived, all that His infinite love has moved Him to provide in Christ Jesus, and that His infinite power, through the Holy Ghost, has made possible to be wrought in sinful man?

Seek this vision from God, and keep it ever before you. Pray the prayer that the apostle Paul prayed for the Ephesian believers, as recorded in Ephesians 1:17, 18, 19, "That the God of our Lord Jesus Christ, the Father of glory, may give unto you a spirit of wisdom and revelation in the knowledge of Him: having the eyes of your heart enlightened, that ye may know what is the hope of His calling, what the riches of the glory of His inheritance in the saints, and what the exceeding greatness of His power to usward who believe."

7

Present-time Blessings

Read with me the first twelve verses of Matthew 5, these verses that we generally call the "Beatitudes." Some tell us that Matthew 5 is a millennial chapter and that we cannot attain to these blessings at the present time. I believe that every one who receives the Baptism in the Spirit has a real foretaste and earnest of millennial blessing, but that here the Lord Jesus is setting forth present-day blessings that we can enjoy here and now.

"Blessed are the poor in spirit: for their's is the kingdom of heaven." This is one of the richest places into which Jesus brings us. The poor have a right to everything in heaven. "Their's is." Dare you believe it? Yes, I dare. I believe, I know, that I was very poor. When God's Spirit comes in as the ruling, controlling power of the life, He gives us God's revelation of our inward poverty, and shows us that God has come with one purpose, to bring heaven's best to earth, and that with Jesus He will indeed "freely give us all things."

An old man and an old woman had lived together for seventy years. Someone said to them, "You must have seen many clouds during those days." They replied, "Where do the showers come from? You never get showers without clouds." It is only the Holy Ghost who can bring us to the place of realization of our poverty; but, every time He does it, He opens the windows of heaven and the showers of blessing fall.

But I must recognize the difference between my own spirit and the Holy Spirit. My own spirit can do certain things on natural lines, can even weep and pray and worship, but it is all on a human plane, and we must not depend on our own human thoughts and activities or on our own personality. If the Baptism means anything to you, it should bring you to the death of the ordinary, where you are no longer putting faith in your own understanding; but, conscious of your own poverty, you are ever yielded to the Spirit. Then it is that your body becomes filled with heaven on earth.

"Blessed are they that mourn: for they shall be comforted." People get a wrong idea of mourning. Over in Switzerland they have a day set apart to take wreaths to graves. I laughed at the people's ignorance and said, "Why are you spending time around the graves? The people you love are not there. All that taking of flowers to the graves is not faith at all." Those who died in Christ are gone to be with Him, "which," Paul said, "is far better."

My wife once said to me, "You watch

me when I'm preaching. I get so near to heaven when I'm preaching that some day I'll be off." One night she was preaching and when she had finished, off she went. I was going to Glasgow and had said goodbye to her before she went to meeting. As I was leaving the house, the doctor and policeman met me at the door and told me that she had fallen dead at the Mission door. I knew she had got what she wanted. I could not weep, but I was in tongues, praising the Lord. On natural lines she was everything to me; but I could not mourn on natural lines, but just laughed in the Spirit. The house was soon filled with people. The doctor said, "She is dead, and we can do no more for her." I went up to her lifeless corpse and commanded death to give her up, and she came back to me for a moment. Then God said to me, "She is Mine; her work is done." I knew what He meant.

They laid her in the coffin, and I brought my sons and my daughter into the room and said, "Is she there?" They said, "No, father." I said, "We will cover her up." If you go mourning the loss of loved ones who have gone to be with Christ, I say it in love to you, you have never had the revelation of what Paul spoke of when he showed us that it is better to go than to stay. We read this in Scripture, but the trouble is that people will not believe it. When you believe God, you will say, "Whatever it is, it is all right. If Thou dost want to take the one I love, it is all right, Lord." Faith removes all tears of self-pity.

But there is a mourning in the Spirit. God will bring you to a place where things must be changed, and there is a mourning, an unutterable groaning until God comes. And the end of all real faith always is re-joicing. Jesus mourned over Jerusalem. He saw the conditions, He saw the unbelief, He saw the end of those who closed their ears to the Gospel. But God gave a promise that He should see the travail of His soul and be satisfied, and that He should see His seed. What happened on the day of Pentecost in Jerusalem was an earnest of what will be the results of His travail, to be multiplied a billionfold all down the ages in all the world. And as we enter in the Spirit into travail over conditions that are wrong, such mourn-ing will ever bring results for God, and our joy will be complete in the satisfaction that is brought to Christ thereby.

"Blessed are the meek: for they shall in-herit the earth." Moses was headstrong in his zeal for his own people, and it resulted in his killing a man. His heart was right in his desire to correct things, but he was working on natural lines, and when we work on nat-ural lines we always fail. Moses had a mighty passion, and that is one of the best things in

the world when God has control and it becomes a passion for souls to be born again;
but apart from God it is one of the worst
things. Paul had it to a tremendous extent,
and, breathing out threatenings, he was hail-
ing men and women to prison. But God
changed it, and later we find him wishing
himself accursed from Christ for the sake
of his brethren, his kinsmen according to the
flesh. God took the headstrong Moses and
molded him into the meekest of men. He
took the fiery Saul of Tarsus and made him
the foremost exponent of grace. Oh, broth-
ers, God can transform you in like manner,
and plant in you a divine meekness and every
other thing that you lack.

In our Sunday school we had a boy with
red hair. His head was as red as fire and so
was his temper. He was such a trial. He
kicked his teachers and the superintendent.
He was simply uncontrollable. The teachers
had a meeting in which they discussed the
matter of expelling him. They thought that
God might undertake for that boy and so
they decided to give him another chance. One
day he had to be turned out, and he broke
all the windows of the mission. He was
worse outside than in. Some time later we
had a ten-days revival meeting. There was
nothing much doing in that meeting and people thought it a waste of time, but there was
one result—the redheaded lad got saved. Aft-

er he was saved, the difficulty was to get rid of him at our house. He would be there until midnight crying to God to make him pliable and use him for His glory. God delivered the lad from his temper and made him one of the meekest, most beautiful boys you ever saw. For twenty years he has been a mighty missionary in China. God takes us just as we are and transforms us by His power.

I can remember the time when I used to go white with rage, and shake all over with temper. I could hardly hold myself together. I waited on God for ten days. In those ten days I was being emptied out and the life of the Lord Jesus was being wrought into me. My wife testified of the transformation that took place in my life, "I never saw such a change. I have never been able to cook anything since that time that has not pleased him. Nothing is too hot or too cold, everything is just right." God must come and reign supreme in your life. Will you let Him do it? He can do it, and He will if you will let Him. It is no use trying to tame the "old man." But God can deal with him. The carnal mind will never be subjected to God, but God will bring it to the cross where it belongs, and will put in its place, the pure, the holy, the meek mind of the Master.

"Blessed are they which do hunger and thirst after righteousness: for they shall be

filled." Note that word, "*shall* be filled."
If you ever see a "shall" in the Bible make it
yours. Meet the conditions and God will
fulfil His word to you. The Spirit of God
is crying, "Ho, every one that thirsteth, come
ye to the waters, and he that hath no money:
come ye, buy and eat; yea, come, buy wine
and milk without money and without price."
The Spirit of God will take of the things
of Christ and show them to you in order that
you may have a longing for Christ in His
fullness, and when there is that longing,
God will not fail to fill you.

See that crowd of worshipers who have
come up to the feast. They are going away
utterly unsatisfied, but on the last day, the
great day of the feast, Jesus stands up and
cries. "If any man thirst, let him come unto me and drink. He that believeth on me, as
the scripture hath said, out of his belly shall
flow rivers of living water." Jesus knew that
they were going away without the living
water, and so He directs them to the true
source of supply. Are you thirsty today?
The living Christ still invites you to Himself,
and I want to testify that He still satisfies
the thirsty soul and still fills the hungry with
good things.

In Switzerland, I learned of a man who
met with the assembly of the Plymouth
Brethren. He attended their various meetings, and one morning, at their breaking of

bread service, he arose and said, "Brethren, we have the Word, and I feel that we are living very much in the letter of it, but there is a hunger and thirst in my soul for something deeper, something more real than we have, and I cannot rest until I enter into it." The next Sunday this brother rose again and said, "We are all so poor here, there is no life in this assembly, and my heart is hungry for reality." He did this for several weeks until it got on the nerves of those people and they protested. "Sands, you are making us all miserable. You are spoiling our meetings, and there is only one thing for you to do, and that is to clear out."

That man went out of the meeting in a very sad condition. As he stood outside, one of his children asked him what was the matter, and he said, "To think that they should turn me out from their midst for being hungry and thirsty for more of God!" I did not know anything of this until afterward.

Some days later someone rushed up to Sands and said, "There is a man over here from England, and he is speaking about tongues and healing." Sands said, "I'll fix him. I'll go to the meeting and sit right up in the front and challenge him with the Scriptures. I'll dare him to preach these things in Switzerland. I'll publicly denounce him."

So he came to the meetings. There he sat. He was so hungry and thirsty that he drank in every word that was said. His opposition soon petered out. The first morning he said to a friend, "This is what I want." He drank and drank of the Spirit. After three weeks he said, "God will have to do something now or I'll burst." He breathed in God and the Lord filled him to such an extent that he spoke in other tongues as the Spirit gave utterance. Sands is now preaching, and is in charge of a new Pentecostal assembly.

God is making people hungry and thirsty after His best. And everywhere He is filling the hungry and giving them that which the disciples received at the very beginning. Are you hungry? If you are, God promises that you shall be filled.